TROWBRIDGE
IN OLD PHOTOGRAPHS

TROWBRIDGE
IN OLD PHOTOGRAPHS

COLLECTED BY
MICHAEL MARSHMAN &
MICHAEL LANSDOWN

ALAN SUTTON
1988
Published in collaboration with

Alan Sutton Publishing Limited
Brunswick Road · Gloucester

First published 1988

British Library Cataloguing in Publication Data

Trowbridge in old photographs.
1. Wiltshire. Trowbridge, history
I. Marshman, Michael
942.3'15

ISBN 0-86299-392-X

Typesetting and origination by
Alan Sutton Publishing Limited.
Printed in Great Britain by
WBC Print Limited.

CONTENTS

INTRODUCTION

Once the largest town in Wiltshire, Trowbridge now ranks third in size although, as it houses the County Council's offices, it has become recognised as the county town. Formerly a market town it was for centuries associated with the manufacture of cloth until the last factory closed down its looms in 1982. Many of its other traditional industries were associated with the countryside – milk, meat, flour and other food products – although light engineering was to become important from the nineteenth century. The surrounding villages had large numbers of people working on the land, although by the twentieth century many were working in the Trowbridge cloth factories and often whole families moved into the town.

This collection of photographs covers the years 1915 to 1959 as a previous work by the compilers has already dealt with the years from 1812 to 1914. It was an era of substantial changes in social, domestic and working life though none so radical as those that were to happen in the following 30 years. Although this period is well remembered by many people still living in the area, even the 1950s now have a remoteness brought about by the rapid advances of the last few decades.

The First World War caused many changes in attitude and brought a desire for better living conditions and amenities which showed itself locally in the council houses built in the 1920s and the slum clearance programmes of the 1930s. The Second World War brought even greater changes and broadened the experience of most local men and women, and again many new houses were built in the post-war years. Although the geographical expansion was considerable, with much farmland being built over, the actual rise in population was very small. The new houses, with gardens, were replacing the small houses built closely together near the town centre where large numbers of people had lived in a very small area.

In the period covered the majority of families had lived in the area for generations and were well known to one another. For many the only times away from the area, apart from war service, were their annual holidays and outings to such places as Weston-super-Mare and Weymouth. This tended to produce a community that was more closely involved in the everyday life of the town where the main news was that of local happenings and many events were organised by, and for, local people.

There must be tens of thousands of photographs covering this period and we have only looked at a fraction of them. Many events and activities have been omitted, although we believe that we have chronicled most of the important events in the area and hopefully have given a glimpse of what life was like during those 50-odd years. Obviously this is only a very superficial picture as, although the best photograph can convey a sense of place, event and time, it can never really show how people lived and felt and what they believed in. Many of the most valuable photographs were never taken; no one pictured grandparents, parents and four children living in a two-bedroomed slum; no one depicted the farm labourer at the end of a ten-hour working day in his draughty leaking cottage; and there are no scenes of the family life of men who were unemployed for years in the 1930s. Most photographs show scenes that people were happy to record and so most collections of old photographs show an unbalanced picture of life.

The bulk of the photographs have come from three collections. Michael Lansdown, when editor of the *Wiltshire Times*, managed to preserve most of the glass negatives that the press photographers had produced from the 1930s to the 1950s; these have now been given to the Wiltshire Library & Museum Service. Charles Marshman began taking photographs around 1930 and most especially captured many events of the 1950s. Ken Rogers recorded the town's buildings, many of which have now been demolished, in the 1950s. Other people, over the years, have loaned or given us photographs which we have used here and we would like to record our thanks to them.

Our greatest expression of thanks goes to Ken Rogers, our fellow Trowbridgian, historian and editor, who has worked closely with us on this book and contributed a great deal in the way of photographs and information. Heartfelt thanks are also due to Michael Randall who had the difficult task of printing nearly half the pictures used from pre-war glass negatives. Wiltshire Library & Museum Service kindly allowed us to use these glass negatives that are now in their possession, while the Wiltshire Record Office provided unfailing help when we were researching the pictures.

The Changing Scene

Until the twentieth century there had been little wholesale demolition of property in Trowbridge although, outside the town, West Ashton village had been removed to create pleasant parkland. During the nineteenth century several courts of poorer buildings were knocked down and replaced with more spacious dwellings and of course many individual houses were demolished to be replaced by something better. In the 1930s the slum clearance programme caused the flattening of houses in many parts of the town and the building of council estates at Shails Lane and Longfield; earlier council estates had been built at Pitman Avenue (1921) and Studley Rise (1929) while rural council houses were built from the early 1920s.

From the late 1920s private housing was built around the main roads: Frome Road, Bradley Road with The Croft and Rutland Crescent, Cockhill and Clarendon Avenue. Further expansion occurred in the 1950s as houses with better amenities were provided, although population growth was slow with an increase of only about 900 between 1939 and 1951. Up to 1959 the town centre changed but little; some new buildings appeared but most remained as they were or were adapted for other uses and trades. The surrounding villages too saw little change and there were few new buildings in the countryside before the 1960s.

CHANGED OUT OF ALL RECOGNITION is this area at what was then (1950s) the top of Duke Street. The basically seventeenth-century and Georgian Duke House, with a conical Victorian entrance with lions on columns, was once the home of the Gouldsmith family, owners of Salter's woollen mills, and it was for a time in the nineteenth century a day and boarding school which also occupied Dorset House in The Halve and the gardens between the two houses. Later it was again a private house, then the premises of the 'Garrick' workmen's club, finally becoming the British Legion Club. Linzey's imposing entrance led to its builder's yard and workshops, filling the area between Duke Street and The Halve. It was the town's top building firm for over 50 years, noted for good design and careful craftsmanship. All this was swept away to open a new road through to The Halve.

ALL THE HOUSES ON THE NORTH SIDE OF DUKE STREET, including a small courtyard called Unity Square, were pulled down during the 1950s and 60s, making way for an extension of Lester's Garage. Some probably dated from the first development of Duke Street in the 1690s, others are early nineteenth-century rebuilding. Note the Cotswold-style stone slates on the roof of the house with the charming bow-windowed, small-paned shop-front. Facing the bottom of Duke Street the Co-op central grocery store had already lost its gabled attic windows but still had its proud inscription in projecting stone letters, cut when the store was built in 1865: 'TROWBRIDGE CO-OPERATIVE INDUSTRIAL AND PROVIDENT SOCIETY LIMITED'. This was laboriously scraped off by the then Co-op authorities in the 1960s as representing an image they wanted to be rid of.

CHING HOUSE, home of woollen manufacturer John Ching in the late eighteenth century, stood in Roundstone Street between Yerbury Street and The Furlong on a site now virtually unrecognizable since construction of the relief road roundabout and underpass and the block of sheltered flats. It stood in front of the Yerbury Street woollen mills, later used for rubber tyre manufacture, and lastly for the production of a patent type of bread.

THESE COTTAGES, of the late seventeenth or early eighteenth century, projected out into Church Street opposite the old Rectory wall and between the parish churchyard and the Manvers Street Methodist Chapel. Their warm old brickwork had acquired a beautiful orange glow, perhaps as a result of earlier colour washing. They were squeezed in between the street and the rear garden walls of the Lloyds and National Provincial banks, and were swept away for street widening in the 1950s.

A HOUSE IN UNION STREET which was no doubt once occupied by a 'respectable' family, but which had sadly come down in the world and was not destined to survive the 1950s. Its fine Regency doorcase would now be a much-admired feature.

FORE STREET, c. 1930, with the Palace Cinema on the right, its entrance flanked by confectionary shops. The George Hotel, on the left, accommodated most visitors as well as hosting the majority of the dinners and dances held in the town.

THE TOWN HALL AND MARKET HALL in the 1950s. As is the case again today the area in front of the Market Hall was used as the chief point of arrival and departure by local bus companies.

ROUNDSTONE STREET in the 1950s before the demolition of the Roundstone Hotel to make way for the present post office. Built in 1865 as the residence and commercial premises of William Applegate, wine merchant, it was a fine example of Victorian design, both decorative and functional, with the large arched windows of the residential block contrasting with the massive fortress-like character of the wine and spirit store.

ONE OF THE HUMBLE, BUT CAREFULLY DESIGNED, STONE FRONTED TERRACES on the west side of Castle Street, which survived into the 1950s but not much longer.

POLEBARN BUILDINGS was a group of eight houses below the entrance to Ashton Street. The houses, apparently built in the late eighteenth century, were in two rows back to back, the only example of this design in Trowbridge. They were pulled down in 1960.

THE HALVE is so-called because it was a 'half-acre' in the common field on this side of the town. After the enclosure of the common fields it remained a long thin ground with a cottage on it until the road was made and houses built from 1784 onwards. These cottages stood at the Hilperton Road end, and one of them may have been the original cottage mentioned in 1752.

SETTLEMENTS AT THE TOWN END OF HILPERTON ROAD were originally cottages built on the waste land. They developed in a variety of styles as the early dwellings were replaced by more substantial houses. The rest of Hilperton Road became the wealthiest area of town being largely built over from the 1820s with Highfield (1859) and Rodwell Hall (1859) both built for clothiers. Other fine stone houses date from the mid-Victorian period although Bellefield House and its park were built c. 1793. In the twentieth century this road was the most attractive approach into the town, passing pleasant dwellings set among mature trees, Bellefield Park and then this interesting line of stone and brick houses, reached where traffic was confined between it and the houses built up to the pavement on the other side of the road. Now, alas, all are gone and after the still attractive earlier part of the road one encounters great emptiness and then a large traffic roundabout.

THE ELEPHANT AND CASTLE remains unchanged, but now it stands all alone surrounded by one of those empty spaces which do so much to disfigure our town. What is now occupied by part of a needlessly large roundabout and a hoarding once provided space for Stainer's Buildings, a handsome stone terrace of clothworkers' houses built in 1830. Opposite this, St Stephen's Place stood where the entrance to the Tesco and multi-storey car-parks now lies. (Lower picture.)

THE TOWN BRIDGE AND WICKER HILL in 1932 show only minor differences to the scene today. Only half the present Pioneer offices had been built and buildings between them and the Parade Commercial Hotel had yet to be demolished for the remaining construction.

AT THE TOP OF WICKER HILL The Parade is here depicted in the early 1940s. The fine Georgian houses are creeper-clad and the pedestrian area in front of them, which had been planted with trees to commemorate Queen Victoria's Jubilee, has been taken over by motor cars.

IN TOWN CENTRES many buildings of interest are hidden away behind the street frontages and can only be seen, and then often not easily, by penetrating courts and back gardens. These tottering structures were revealed when buildings in Church Street, on the site (still empty) adjoining the Halifax Building Society, were cleared in 1960, and disappeared themselves soon after. They were built as clothiers' workshops in the late eighteenth century, and may have held spinning jennies.

ANOTHER BEHIND-THE-STREET SCENE, and a building happily still with us. This is the rear wing of the late medieval building opposite the end of Church Walk in Church Street, which itself probably dates from Tudor times. The whole group is being restored at the time of writing. Excavations in this garden in 1988 have suggested that members of the Fox family, known to have been tobacco pipemakers in the seventeenth and early eighteenth centuries and to have lived on this estate, actually carried on their business here as well.

SILVERTHORNE'S COURT, now a litter-strewn pathway between Roundstone Street and Duke Street, was a terrace of nine cottages built in the early eighteenth century. Known to older Trowbridge people as 'The Drung' (a dialect word for a passage), its houses were condemned in 1937, but the two shown in these pictures were unaccountably left until 1962.

KNEE'S CORNER STORE was a familiar landmark in Fore Street, at the entrance to Church Walk. In November 1935 the Tudor timber-framed house was demolished. There was a body of opinion that felt the site should remain open to provide a pleasing view of the parish church, but the rather bleak Burton's shop (now Fosters) was built instead.

A DISASTROUS FIRE broke out in Knee's department store on 15 November 1940. Property and stock worth thousands of pounds were destroyed with most of the damage occurring in the area fronting Castle Street.

THE CORNER OF TIMBRELL STREET AND PROSPECT PLACE shows an interesting contrast. In Timbrell Street the design of the houses was uniform, all the windows being sashed, whereas in Prospect Place the houses varied in height and in design. The group above has casements on the upper floors which were used for weaving shops, while in between is a warehouse, probably built in mid-Victorian times. It was used by one of several marine-store dealers who bought rags, bones and metal for recycling.

THIS PRETTY PAIR OF TUDOR VILLAS were also in Prospect Place, and were the only houses in this part of the town with any pretensions to gentility.

THOMAS STREET, named after Thomas Timbrell, ran from Prospect Place to Charlotte Street across the site now occupied by Charlotte Court. Unlike Timbrell Street, the house frontages were not uniform, and evidently the purchasers of individual plots had houses built to their own requirements – if they were weavers they needed a top-floor workshop, but if factory workers they did not.

CROSS STREET joined Timbrell Street and Charlotte Street. On the inner (town) side was a group of quite prosperous houses, sometimes called Timbrell Place, which had gardens in front stretching through to Timbrell Street and their backs to Cross Street, as shown here.

TIMBRELL STREET was constructed across open land in 1814 to provide an entrance to the town from Staverton and Holt which was better than the narrow Frog Lane. This uniform terrace occupied a large part of the east side above the entrance to Cross Street to the left. It was demolished in 1971, ruining what had been a handsome street.

THE BRICK PLAT, the old name of three rows of houses at right angles to Union Street opposite the end of the Halve. One row which survived until the early 1960s was later called St Thomas's Passage. The houses were built in the mid-eighteenth century and were the earliest examples of the three-storeyed clothworkers' houses in the town.

ISLINGTON originated as cottages built on the verges near the entrance to the Down, then a common. One early house, shown in the centre in the top picture, survives, but the two seen side on, which were also much older than their frontage suggested, have gone. The rest of the road was filled by terrace houses in the early nineteenth century, of which the groups near the Down still stand. The archway leads to a group of buildings once used as clothiers' workshops by Samuel Pitman (father of Sir Isaac, inventor of Pitman's shorthand), and later used for making horse rugs before becoming a dairy.

IN THE PARISH CHURCHYARD stood this small stone house, once associated with Sir Isaac Pitman, that had several other buildings for company until they were pulled down in 1859. This one survived only to be destroyed by fire.

THE HORSE TROUGH IN BYTHESEA ROAD had been erected by Samuel Bythesea for the coronation of Edward VII in 1902. It was never connected with a piped water supply and relied upon rainwater to fill it. By March 1937 it was deemed to be a traffic obstruction and it was demolished that year.

THE CAMERA SUGGESTS A WIDER EXPANSE OF ROAD in Stallard Street than was really the case in the 1950s. The house and shop, this side of The Rose and Crown, have been replaced by office buildings.

TRINITY VILLAS, seen here in the 1920s, were part of an interesting group with Trinity Church and School and St George's Terrace, all built in the 1830s and 1840s. By the 1950s the villas housed a doctor's surgery but later they were among many fine houses demolished to make way for the Trowbridge Inner Relief Road.

THE WOOLPACK, which with the George was one of Trowbridge's principal inns, stood from the early eighteenth century on the site of that part of Knee's which faces the Midland Bank. The yard behind stretched through to Castle Street and these three brick houses, with an archway to allow coaches and wagons access, were built there in 1797. Their demolition a few years ago created another of those open spaces which have had such a disastrous visual effect on parts of our town centre.

VISITORS TO TROWBRIDGE are often puzzled by the name of Bythesea Road. It comes from a family who were prosperous in the town for a couple of centuries from about 1660. Henry Bythesea, a clothier who lived in Bridge House, built a complex of small houses adjoining Stallard Street in the 1790s. Most were swept away when Bythesea Road was constructed in 1894, but these survived until 1988.

IN THE YEARS AFTER 1790, machinery for most of the processes of the woollen industry came into general use and Trowbridge began to expand rapidly. Although weaving continued to be done by hand for another 70 years, there was now incentive for weavers to settle in the town close to the factories they wove for, and several hundred houses of the type shown here, with top-floor weaving shops, were built between 1790 and 1830. These stood at the upper end of Bradford Road and were demolished in the late 1950s.

A TERRACE OF THREE-STOREYED WEAVERS' HOUSES still stands in Newtown, but another, between that and the end of Gloucester Road, was demolished in pre-war slum clearance. The site has never been re-used, except for a row of advertisement hoardings.

MANY STREET CORNERS POSSESSED A SHOP. This one was in a pleasant stone house in Dursley Road at the junction with Mortimer Street and was one of the many small shops serving that part of the town. The photographer caught by the camera is Peter Maundrell who was engaged in recording parts of Trowbridge before they were demolished.

STILL STANDING IN THE LATE 1950s was this brick terrace in Mortimer Street opposite the entrance to Dursley Road. To the right are the Co-operative Stores and The Greyhound; today The Greyhound alone remains on this side of the whole length of Mortimer Street.

IN THE WEEK OF 1 October 1938, when Mr Hore Belisha, Secretary of State for War, was opening the new Tank Corps Barracks at Warminster, these soldiers were engaged on a seemingly unwarlike task. Men from the Royal Horse Artillery Barracks were engaged in assisting the Urban District Council by demolishing these stone houses in Frome Road that had been condemned as slums. This work would however be good experience when dealing with the bomb-damaged houses that would soon become all too common in the country. Perhaps as a public relations exercise the soldiers are wearing their gas masks; it was also in this week that masks were distributed to a slightly mistrustful public. The houses, like many in the town, were condemned because of the poor living conditions and lack of amenities. If they still existed today it would doubtless be possible to renovate them and provide comfortable homes.

WHEN THE RAILWAY WAS LAID AT A SLIGHTLY HIGHER LEVEL THAN DURSLEY ROAD, the drains under it were inadequate to carry storm water away in a really heavy downpour, and so the lowest point of the road (where Rutland Crescent joins it) was regularly flooded. The houses on the right were part of a row of eight houses at right angles to the road, known to Lower Studleyites as the Side Rank, now replaced by bungalows.

THIS VIEW OF WEST ASHTON ROAD was taken before the building of Clarendon Avenue. The field on which it stands was bought by the Town Council from the Rood Ashton estate. The idea of building council houses on the site was abandoned, and the present private houses were named Clarendon Avenue in 1933.

MANY OF THE OLD COTTAGES in the formerly rural parts of Trowbridge were built on pieces of roadside verge enclosed by 'squatters' under the erroneous, but widespread, belief that, if a house could be begun at dawn and have smoke rising from its chimney at sunset, it was legally the property of the builder. Both pictures show groups of houses which appeared in this way, though the actual buildings are probably not the original ones.

The small house in Holbrook Lane was the town's last but one thatched house. At this time (the 1950s) the lane was still to some extent a country one, though the Studley Rise houses backed on to it at one end and at the other end The Croft and associated houses appeared before the war. The lower picture shows cottages at Upper Studley.

ONE OF THE MOST FREQUENTLY FLOODED AREAS IN TROWBRIDGE was the land around Cradle Bridge. This picture from the early 1950s shows buildings that have now totally vanished; only part of the garden wall of Longfield House remains today.

THE HILPERTON INSTITUTE was completely destroyed by fire in July 1939, the remains being chiefly corrugated iron. Besides the loss of a valuable community resource the village lost two billiard tables, a piano and a stage with new scenery.

World Wars and the Military

The men of the Royal Horse Artillery left Trowbridge Barracks to go to war on 5 August 1914, while in October the town became the recruiting and training headquarters for the newly formed 2/4th Battalion of the Wiltshire Regiment. Various other battalions were billeted in the town and from September 1914 Belgian refugees were given shelter for the rest of the war. Around 2,600 men from Trowbridge and many hundreds from local villages served in the armed forces; of 179 from Steeple Ashton 30 were not to return while an eighth of the townsmen were killed.

After the Armistice the 'L' Battalion of the Royal Horse Artillery, who fought heroically defending Néry against overwhelming odds, returned to the barracks. The town erected its War Memorial in the park and settled back to enjoy peace. In less than 20 years air raid shelters were being built, gas masks distributed, trenches dug and ARP wardens trained as the country entered the era of the Munich Agreement. When war came the town was emptied of young men and women as Trowbridgians went off to fight; their place was taken by some 3,000 evacuees who were billeted in the town and villages. Apart from billeting, Home Guard and ARP duties, the local war effort included scrap metal collection, vegetable growing, raising money to pay for an aircraft and of course war work which included building parts for Spitfires. Trowbridge was lucky and suffered few bombs and only one damaging raid.

KING GEORGE V AND QUEEN MARY talking to wounded soldiers during their visit to Trowbridge in 1917 when they met local notabilities in the Town Hall and also inspected war supply manufacture in local factories.

A COMPANY OF AUSTRALIAN SOLDIERS, seen lined up in the station yard, gave a fine display of physical drill and staged a mock battle in the Flower Show Field in September 1917. Sound effects from mortars and rifles were appreciated by a large crowd and a collection was made to provide funds for Wiltshire prisoners of war.

THE ARMISTICE WAS SIGNED at 5.00 a.m. on 11 November 1918 and all hostilities ceased at 11.00 a.m. When this became known all work came to a halt in Trowbridge and thousands of thankful people flocked to the town centre. At 1.30 p.m. the Revd Harry Saunders gave a short address from the balcony of the Town Hall and cheers were given for the king and the 'boys'. In the evening most of the townspeople assembled laughing and singing for a joyous lantern procession.

THE BRITISH TANK which was brought to Trowbridge in December 1919 became a favourite play-spot for boys in the corner of the park between the War Memorial and the market before it was broken up for scrap in 1940. The tank, No. 222, Mark IV type, had taken part in the 1917 battles of Arras, Ypres Salient and Messines and was one of the 500 tanks that played a great part in the Allied offensive at Cambrai on 20 November 1917.

IN OUR PRESENT-DAY WORLD OF CONTINUOUS NOISE it becomes difficult to imagine the strict observation of the Silence at 11.00 a.m. on Armistice Day. Whatever work was taking place would cease: vehicles would stop, drivers and passengers dismount, children and babies would be hushed. Everyone would stand with bowed heads remembering the carnage of the Great War that had left few families untouched, remembering those who remained in Flanders' fields or beneath some cold ocean, remembering those who returned gassed, blinded or maimed.

In Trowbridge on 11 November 1937 some 400 people attended the service at the War Memorial where, among the wreaths and flowers, was an immense emblem of silken poppies and golden leaves from businesses, organisations and schools and known simply as the 'town's wreath'. Some 308 young men of Trowbridge died during that war; many would have been remembered by the driver of this Great Western Railway vehicle.

THE ARMISTICE DAY SERVICE was attended by a crowd which was only about half the size of those in previous years in 1935. This photograph used infra-red photography to record the scene, thereby eliminating the November haze and fog but turning the grass white.

A SCENE FROM ARMISTICE DAY in the 1950s, with the British Legion Parade led by veterans of the First World War. Their route took them alongside the Market House and through the Market Yard on their way to the War Memorial in the park.

THE TROWBRIDGE BRANCH OF THE OLD CONTEMPTIBLES from the First World War received a new standard in August 1936. At the War Memorial the standard is blessed by the Revd T.A. Bold, chaplain to the local branch. Holding the standard is Brigadier General H. Lewin, who took the salute and march past, while behind the table is Captain T.C. Usher who made the presentation.

THE TROWBRIDGE DIVISION OF THE WHITE ENSIGN ASSOCIATION were presented with a new standard by Admiral Ellerton on Sunday 9 June 1940. After the dedication at Holy Trinity Church, 35 members of the Association with 30 Old Contemptibles and 60 members of the British Legion marched to the barracks accompanied by troops of the ATS and the Band of the Church Lads Brigade.

IN THE ROYAL HORSE ARTILLERY SPORTS in June 1933 the soldiers demonstrate the art of bareback riding in both senses of the phrase.

THESE MEN WERE BEING TRAINED IN THE USE OF MECHANISED TRANSPORT by January 1938. Pictured at the barracks are the different types of vehicle in use. On the left is the 'Dragon' which was used to pull guns. It had a 90 horse power engine and did three to four miles to the gallon. The mechanisation was complete by the summer of 1938.

MR PHILIP M. SNAILUM auctions 40 of the horses of 'L' Néry Battery of the Royal Horse Artillery in November 1937 as, less than two years before the outbreak of World War II, the battery had been mechanised. The firm of auctioneers were more usually found at the livestock market or at various farm sales, but on this occasion had erected a temporary rostrum at Trowbridge Barracks.

WHEN WAR CAME many people found themselves carrying out tasks that they would never have dreamed of undertaking in peace time. In 1940 schoolboy Norman Butcher, 12-year-old son of Trowbridge ARP instructor Mr W.G. Butcher, was tired of games and reading so he started knitting for the war effort. He quickly completed a pair of socks and was busy on a scarf.

FOR THE CORONATION OF KING GEORGE VI the men of 'L' Battery of the Royal Horse Artillery naturally wore their full dress uniform. They are pictured before taking part in the day's local ceremonies.

THE FUNERAL OF LANCE SERGEANT NORRISH of the Royal Horse Artillery on 20 March 1939 was the first military funeral in Trowbridge since the battery had been mechanised. For the first time the hearse was pulled by a tractor lorry rather than horses.

THIS OLD BUS, with its Irish registration number, was converted into the Wiltshire ARP Mobile School and is depicted in June 1938. It toured villages giving people instruction in air raid precautions.

At this time it was estimated that Trowbridge needed 500 volunteers in the event of war; there were less than 100. Parish and town councils were distributing gas masks although some of these were not assembled and many people had not been trained in their use. The ARP headquarters was at the Town Hall and it had been decided that the air raid alarm would be the siren at the gasworks. Provision was made for first aid posts, air raid wardens, the ambulance and fire services, rescue and first aid parties and decontamination squads as, in October, Trowbridge paid little heed to the Munich Agreement of 30 September.

THE MILITARY became established on Salisbury Plain at the end of the nineteenth century and their presence had considerable effects on many local towns and villages. In Trowbridge, apart from the sounds of gunfire and mortars, the most noticeable effect was that of convoys of troops passing through the town.

On Tuesday 14 September 1937, 290 tanks were engaged on manoeuvres from Tilshead and several of them passed through Trowbridge. This one has stopped in Frome Road outside Holy Trinity (later Park Street) School and is providing the schoolchildren with a close up view of life in the British Army.

PART OF THE ORIGINAL CAVALRY BARRACKS OF 1794 pictured in the 1950s shortly before demolition. Cavalry had been used in the town during the Chartist disturbances of 1839, but in the twentieth century the barracks housed a battalion of the Royal Horse Artillery who by 1938 had lost their horses.

VARIOUS DRIVES FOR SCRAP METAL, to be turned into aeroplanes, tanks and guns, gradually denuded the country of most non-essential metallic objects. One result was that very few iron railings survived this part of the war effort. Local papers published figures of the amounts of different metals that had been collected that week; in July 1940 the WVS organised an aluminium collection that brought in 15¾ hundredweight of scrap.

In the picture Mr Holloway's lorry is loaded high by enthusiastic volunteers outside the Town Hall.

OVER THE FIRST WEEKEND IN SEPTEMBER 1939 nearly 3,000 women, children and blind people were received into Trowbridge homes as evacuees. All except the blind were in private houses causing a revolution in the domestic and social lives of nearly everyone in the area. These pictures show several hundred children, with gas masks and labels, arriving at Trowbridge station on Friday 2 September before they walked to reception centres or were driven to their new homes. A holiday atmosphere prevailed, some children having their very first ride in a motor car and most local homes welcoming the evacuees. The following Monday, normally a quiet day when shops redressed their windows, was very busy with crowded shops and streets as the newcomers explored.

EVACUEES FROM LONDON were totally inexperienced in the ways of the country and a country town and various acclimatisation exercises were mounted. This party visited Wyke Farm in September 1939 where, among other facts of life, they learned that milk came from cows rather than glass bottles or metal churns. While the children observe Mr Stone, the farmer, milking a cow, a nice touch of humour is provided by the white farmyard cat watching the milk with a look of anticipation. The children also met the bull, in his pen, and were given apples from the orchard. In the background of both views are the nineteenth-century cattle stalls. Some evacuees quickly adapted to rural life and were given their own area in The Halve for allotments where they produced food for the war effort.

A SPECIAL ONE-DAY EXCURSION TRAIN brought 120 mums, dads, brothers and sisters from London to visit the Trowbridge evacuees on 17 December 1939. Despite the biting east wind, joy and laughter prevailed at the railway station and parents were surprised at the healthy effects of country life on their youngsters. Volunteers had laid on a fleet of cars and there were impromptu parties in many homes that day.

AS MEN JOINED THE ARMED FORCES, more and more jobs were taken over by women. The first four women porters in Trowbridge, Mesdames Vosper, Cooper, Holmes and Glasspool, are pictured with the station foreman, Mr L. Steele.

A DEFENCE BILL WAS INTRODUCED in 1939 that placed a statutory obligation on employers of more than 50 people to provide their employees with air raid shelters. At Clark's Studley Mill on 27 April 1939 the brainchild of Mr Albert Lester was unveiled – shelters constructed from disused boilers, each of which would hold 75 people.

OWING TO WARTIME CENSORSHIP the locations of enemy actions could not be published, but we believe this to be the scene after a bomb had fallen either at Hilperton Marsh or Semington. There was a crater 25 ft. across and 12 ft. deep and the explosion affected nine dwellings. One pig was killed and about 100 fowls were blown to pieces, but horses a few yards from the crater were unharmed and there were no human casualties.

THE 66 OFFICERS AND MEN OF TROWBRIDGE FIRE SERVICE, under their Commandant Mr E.G. Reynolds, carried out fire fighting exercises at the Town Bridge in 1941. In the top picture is their new Leyland fire engine, which had been put into service on 4 June at a cost of £148, outside the entrance to Kemp & Hewitt's Innox Mill.

The lower picture is especially interesting as it shows the section of Bridge House that was destroyed by bombs in 1942. A tower, possibly for a staircase, can be seen to the right of the water jets.

BRITISH TANK '222' arrived in Trowbridge from the battlefields of France on 18 December 1919. In its difficult passage through the town it nearly demolished the Town Bridge before being set on the site of the present War Memorial. When this was built in 1921 the tank was moved to its final resting place in the park nearer to Castle Street. In 1940 it was decided to cut up the tank for scrap metal to aid the war effort. At the same time the nearby drinking fountain was replaced by a new one.

BESIDES COLLECTING VARIOUS COMMODITIES FOR THE WAR EFFORT money was raised by a variety of means. In 1941 War Weapons Week gave Trowbridge a target of £100,000. On the morning of Saturday 26 April Mr A. Batley was able to stand on the balcony of the Town Hall and proudly announce a total of £246,764. By that evening Mr C. Ingham Haden was able to report that this had risen to £267,398 – an average of £22 5s.0d. (£22.25) for each person in the town.

WVS LADIES were busy making camouflage nets near the main entrance to Trowbridge Park in October 1940.

THIS HANDSOME JERSEY COW from South Wraxall was to be found in the Market Yard collecting funds for the local farmers' Red Cross effort in September 1941.

EXPONENTS OF THE SLOGAN 'DIG FOR VICTORY' had, in 1941, dug up the lawns in front of County Hall and grown a fine crop of onions. In April 1942 members of the Woman's Land Army dug the ground with the assistance of Mr D. Harris, the County Horticultural Officer, (bending on the left) and Mr W.T. Price, the County Agricultural Organiser (far right). In the lower picture the raised flower beds are planted with vegetables to produce a decorative effect using red-leafed beetroot, dwarf beans, red cabbage, leeks and carrots. Members of County Hall staff tended the growing crops which, when mature, were used in the canteen.

A 'SEVERE AIR RAID' WAS SIMULATED with a total of 23 separate incidents on Sunday 17 January 1940. It revealed great efficiency as 56 casualties were rescued and treated. Pictured is the fire fighting scene at the bottom of Wicker Hill where 'high explosive bombs' had fallen on the Town Bridge Garage. It was in this area that German bombs were to fall in 1942 killing two people at Bridge House and demolishing the top floor of The Bear Inn.

ANOTHER ARP EXERCISE on 3 March 1940 in Thomas Street was watched by Colonel Carlisle, the Regional Director. An injured man is strapped to a board and lowered from an upper floor thus providing local people with some welcome wartime entertainment.

A NATIONAL DAY OF PRAYER was designated on Sunday 8 September 1940, both in this country and the USA. The Home Guard, the recently renamed Local Defence Volunteers, are led by Major Eric MacKay along Stallard Street after attending service at Holy Trinity Church.

A SPLENDID VIEW OF CASTLE STREET as it was in the 1940s shows what we believe to be the Remembrance Day Parade of 1940.

Church, Chapel and the Big House

Like most market towns Trowbridge was blessed with many churches and chapels, while each village had its church and often one or more chapels. It was doubtless the woollen industry that gave rise to the strong nonconformist attitudes of the area with Methodist, Baptist, Unitarian and Congregational chapels. All four of the town's present Anglican churches and the Roman Catholic church attracted good congregations throughout the period and much of the social life of the town was organised through the different churches and their Sunday schools.

Most of the grander houses had been built by clothiers and several, such as Courtfield House (the MacKays) and Bellefield House (the Clarks) were still occupied by factory owners. The only house in the area which would have qualified as a stately home today was Rood Ashton Hall, built by the Long family. Although never owning land in the town they were regarded as the local squires of Trowbridge and were involved in many local activities and ceremonies.

THE TWELVE BELLS OF ST JAMES' PARISH CHURCH laid out on the churchyard path ready for hoisting to the belfry in the summer of 1934. Prominent in these pictures, extreme right in both, is Sam Hector, for many years captain of the bellringers. The original eight bells had been increased to ten by adding two war memorial bells after the First World War. In 1934 they needed re-hanging and it was decided to increase the peal to twelve. A town fund-raising campaign was a great success; each bell was 'adopted' by an individual or a local organisation. The tenor bell, seen ready for hoisting, was adopted by the directors, staff and employees of Usher's Brewery and was named the 'T.C. Usher Bell' after the then chairman of the brewery. Ushers also named their new pub, at the top of Shails Lane, the Twelve Bells.

THE LESS PICTURESQUE EARLY NINETEENTH-CENTURY EXTENSION OF THE OLD RECTORY, with one end of the earlier, stone-built, gabled, mullioned Parsonage, with Georgian sash windows replacing the older ones. The poet George Crabbe, rector from 1814 to 1832, wrote many of his later poems in the study lit by these windows and through all his 18 years in Trowbridge until his death, aged 78, was struggling to pay off the debt incurred by his predecessor in building the extension. After much heart searching and agonized debate during the 1950s, the church people decided they must, with deep regret, pull down the inconvenient old building; it was replaced in the early 1960s by the present new Rectory, church hall and car-park.

THE IMPOSING BULK OF NORTH BRADLEY RECTORY, seen from the top of the church tower in 1950. The Rectory, built in early Victorian times, had extensive views over empty fields.

EMMANUEL CHURCH celebrated the bicentenary of its founding in Back Street (now Church Street) on Sunday 4 October 1936. One of the events organised by local Baptists was this rally addressed by the Minister of Emmanuel, the Revd W.G. Owen, in Witch Pit Wood, Southwick.

Witch Pit Wood has an honoured place in the history of nonconformity locally for it was here, in a natural dell in the middle of the wood, that Baptists met in the 1660s when there were several Acts of Parliament passed against them and they were hunted out by informers. The wood was on the Cutteridge Estate owned by Mr William Trenchard, a Member of Parliament and a justice of the peace who was a zealous dissenter. He gave shelter and protection to the worshippers and most probably used his influence to protect them from fines and imprisonment. Often the church met at night and in 1669 between two and three hundred people were in the dell at a time, invisible until a walker was literally on top of them.

THE OPEN AIR BAPTISTRY AT SOUTHWICK BAPTIST CHAPEL had been in use for two centuries in 1910 but, after that year, baptisms ceased owing to the polluted nature of the stream that supplied the baptistry. After several years of planning it was restored and re-opened on 22 September 1937 when many people from West Wiltshire, and indeed from a large number of Baptist churches in the south-west, were present.

The day was also the eightieth birthday of one of the oldest members of the local congregation, Mrs Caroline Doel, who had been baptised in the pool some six decades earlier. The work of restoration was undertaken by the Hon. Treasurer of the Baptist Association, Mr A.R. Linzey, at cost price.

Money was raised by a Two Thousand Shillings Fund (putting the cost at £100) with appeals throughout the Western Area of Baptist Churches. Southwick made the first contribution with 275 shillings and by the time of the re-opening 800 shillings had been raised; a further £10 was collected from the large assembly taking the total to the halfway mark.

Southwick was one of the earliest centres of Baptist activity and a church is known to have existed there as early as 1655 although the present chapel was built in 1815.

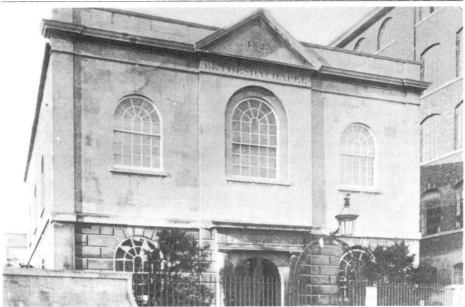

THE PARTICULAR BAPTIST CHURCH which met in Bethesda Chapel had been formed in 1821 with just 18 members. The chapel was built in 1823 at a cost of £2,200 and could seat 860 people with an upper gallery for 300 children. Pictured in the 1920s before the 1931 fire at the adjacent Home Mills damaged the building.

A PICTURE TAKEN AFTER THE OPENING OF THE GLOUCESTER ROAD BETHESDA CHAPEL on 18 March 1931. The building was designed by Trowbridge architect Mr W.W. Snailum and opened by Mrs E.W. Brown.

THE TABERNACLE CHURCH removed these early houses in 1937, one of which had been a bookshop that fronted Church Street. By this time there was also a builder's yard and workshop on the site. The scheme was initiated by W. Nelson Haden and C. Ingham Haden, who also paid for it, and by February 1938 this rose garden had been created. The demolition was the forerunner of the further destruction of the street line in this part of Church Street which was continued so effectively in the 1950s and 1960s.

THE BETHESDA SUNDAY SCHOOL, marching up Wicker Hill into Fore Street, in company with other Sunday Schools in the town on the occasion of the Silver Jubilee of King George V in 1935.

THE RECTOR OF HILPERTON, the Revd D.C.C. Dunlop, revived the Rogation Service in the village, holding it on the allotments in Middle Lane on Sunday 17 May 1936.

THIS IS THE FUNERAL OF EDMUND ASHBY of Spiers Piece Farm, Steeple Ashton, at the church there in October 1935. Aged 74, he had lived at the farm since 1869 and was regarded as the father of the parish to whom anyone could go for help or advice. His life had been full — sergeant in the Yeomanry, keen sportsman, leading figure in agricultural affairs, JP, chairman for many years of the RDC, the Board of Guardians, the Trowbridge branch of the NFU and the parish council.

He kept a large staff on the farm, believing that men who had worked well until they were over 60 should be able to take things a bit more easily in their last years at work.

SPRINGFIELD HOUSE, just before its demolition in 1958. Only the gate piers at the town end of Springfield Park, in Hilperton Road, and a few fine specimen trees are left to remind us of this great mansion and its spacious grounds. Built around 1840 in the 'Italianate' style characteristic of the early Victorian period, it was the home of William Stancomb, woollen manufacturer, Lord of the Manor and builder of Trowbridge Market House in 1862, who later moved to an even grander home at Blount's Court, Potterne. Springfield's last occupants were Mr J.G. Gramlick, a retired manufacturer from Austria, and his two unmarried daughters; by their time the house and its contents had become very dilapidated. Sadly no detailed record was made of its appearance before it succumbed to site redevelopment.

THESE DEER AT BELLEFIELD PARK are on the site of what is now Stancomb Avenue. Bellefield House had been owned by Major Thomas Clark who caused a local sensation by marrying a girl, from his own cloth factory, who was nearly 30 years his junior. In times of hardship in the 1930s Mrs Dorcas Clark would send the carcase of a deer to the Trowbridge soup kitchen. In March 1938 the roe deer were offered to anyone who would provide a good home as the park was to be sold for housing development.

DESIGNED BY JEFFERY WYATT, Rood Ashton Hall was built for the Long family in 1808. In 1923 it was recorded that it had always been the rule on the estate that tenant farmers were succeeded by their sons, or failing a son the tenant could nominate his successor. The Longs spent much money in farming experiments and improvements but the estates were sold some decades before this picture of the western side of the derelict Hall was taken, c. 1957.

THE DERELICT ROOD ASHTON HALL was surrounded by pastureland which supported dairy cattle in the 1950s. Seeking a place to deposit the by-products of his cattle, farmer Fred Corp found the ideal situation on the hard standing at the grand entrance to the Hall. Thus the area where Walter Long, First Lord of the Admiralty, was often photographed was piled high with dung.

WALTER LONG died in 1924 and the estate was broken up, the mansion being sold in 1930. It was used by the services during World War II and then sold again in 1950 when it was stripped of most of its fittings including the roof. This once fine ceiling is pictured c. 1958.

AFTER THE DEATH OF THEIR DAUGHTER, Margaret, Mr and Mrs Bernard Caillard opened Wingfield House as a Church of England Waifs and Strays Home in her memory. The opening and dedication was performed by the Duchess of Beaufort on 31 October 1935. This chapel was created in the house and five dormitories and many other facilities were provided.

BEFORE ADCROFT HOUSE BECAME THE PRESENT TROWBRIDGE HOSPITAL in 1929 it was home to the Rodway family. The Georgian mansion had 6½ acres of grounds laid out as pleasant gardens. In the cool greenhouse orchids were grown with *Dendrobium nobile* and *Coelogyne cristata* in the baskets and a *Cattleya* over the asparagus beds.

COURTFIELD HOUSE was the home of clothiers from at least 1752 when John Cockes bought, re-modelled and extended it. Despite being close to its cloth factories it had large pleasant gardens and orchards, partly seen in this view of the back of the house. It maintained its connection with clothiers until well after World War II when the MacKays (of Palmer & MacKays) lived there. The back part of the house appears to be the oldest, and it is probable that John Cockes refronted the existing house in brick. Some of the lower, earlier parts are of stone and, to the east, there are weaver's windows that would have allowed handlooms to be worked on the top floor. Cockes also built the two-storey workshops that still adjoin the house to the west. Further west there is a large single-storey wool warehouse built between 1840 and 1860.

RUTLAND HOUSE was probably built about the same time as the adjoining barracks, in 1794, and may have been for the commanding officer. It was pulled down in 1963 to make way for the new filling station of what was then Ramseyer Motors, now Kirkby Ford Motors. By this time the Bradley Road area had developed dramatically from 1794 when, apart from the Barracks and Rutland House, the only dwellings were a few small cottages in Bradley Road, opposite the entrance to The Croft, Holbrook Lane and Silver Street Lane. Ribbon development began in the late nineteenth century at the Frome Road end and continued southwards until Holbrook Lane was reached c. 1930. The areas of The Croft and Rutland Crescent were then built over.

SECTION FOUR

The Conigre

Building in this area had begun in the second half of the seventeenth century with cottages of stone rubble, mullioned windows and drip moulds. The area had been occupied by reasonably prosperous tradesmen during the first half of the eighteenth century and there were some good large houses around the edges. By the end of that century houses had become densely packed in the area bounded by Shails Lane, Upper Broad Street, Conigre and Back Street, and the lack of water and abundance of cess pits caused a great decline in living standards. From the late eighteenth century the area was the chief slum of the town, a distinction it enjoyed until its demolition.

Respectable people did not go into the Conigre, policemen tended to visit in pairs when investigating one of the petty crimes of its numerous inhabitants and the landlords who extracted considerable sums in rent for the hovels sent in hired rent collectors. A sink of iniquity which bred most of the diseases suffered in the town (in the 1860s Frog Lane had an open sewer in which small children doubtless sailed home-made boats) or a community where life was passionate and full blooded? Certainly the children had rickets, there was stench and squalor, the common lodging house kept busy and men would drink their week's pay, yet at times there was colour, vivacity and humour.

By the 1930s the writing was on the wall for the Conigre as houses all over the town were condemned as slums. There were protests, from tenants as well as landlords, but the 'Conigre Crowd' of 100-odd families were rehoused on the estate known by the pleasant field name of Gooseacre. This quickly became known as Chinatown and is now called the Seymour Estate. The Urban Council demolished the slums but then paused and a contemporary report spoke of the 'ghastly appearance' and the aspect of a 'giant rockery'. Final demolition did not take place until the 1950s and since then the area has been used for a bus station and car-parks. Its appearance strikes many as being far worse than when it was full of seventeenth- and eighteenth-century dwellings.

THE FINE SEVENTEENTH- AND EIGHTEENTH-CENTURY BUILDINGS of the Conigre were regarded as the town's worst slum by 1934, with shared lavatories and kitchens which acted as coal cellars, larders, bathrooms and clothes drying areas. The mood of the times was to rehouse the families in new council housing and demolish the old buildings.

THE SECOND WORLD WAR interrupted the Urban Council's slum clearance and these houses remained until the 1950s. The once close-knit community, where many townspeople would fear to walk, was completely destroyed, roads disappeared and the area was given over to car-parking and the bus station.

NOTHING REMAINS of the houses and shops that once housed about 150 familes in the Conigre, site of the bus station (now itself closed and derelict). Demolition as part of the later town's enthusiastic slum clearance campaign took place from 1934, but a few buildings including the one on the right in the lower picture (a bakery and shop with dormer windows) survived into the 1950s. In 1936 the UDC Chairman, Perkins Garlick, boasted that nearly 500 dwellings had been condemned and one-seventh of the population rehoused by the Council and the Conservative Minister of Health held Trowbridge up as an example he hoped other towns would quickly copy.

ONLY ONE FEATURE REMAINS on these two pictures to guide people to their location – the tank on the top of Usher's Back Street brewery in the top picture. The viewpoint of that picture is near Westcroft, so that now we should have the British Row part of Usher's on our left and the open spaces of the Conigre on our right.

THE LOWER PICTURE IS TAKEN IN THE OTHER DIRECTION, so that Westcroft is just round the corner at the top end. The buildings on the left were between Frog Lane and the street (at a higher level) called the Conigre. A flight of stone steps joined the two levels near Westcroft. The whole area was changed to its present form in 1963.

The building nearest the camera was a cottage given to the town as a soup kitchen (i.e. to provide soup for poor families in times of distress) in 1888 and last used in 1936.

THIS PICTURE from the 1950s shows not only a well-maintained and habitable Conigre Parsonage, but also the fine three-storeyed building that housed the printers, Diplocks, in Upper Broad Street. The road between the two houses went to The Beeches as it still does today. These three houses, with Westcroft, were typical of the fine houses built at the edge of the town's worst slum. The inhabitants would have found nothing incongruous in this, at a time when beauty co-existed with ugliness and wealth with deprivation.

Until the nineteenth century, virtually all the town's clothiers lived near the centre, close to their workshops and factories; often with houses and small courts built at the bottom of their gardens.

Conigre Parsonage had been given by the Houlton family, who developed the Conigre, as the residence for the minister of the Conigre Chapel; sadly, in the 1970s and 1980s the Parsonage was allowed to become derelict and is one of the buildings most commented on by visitors to the town.

NOWADAYS it is difficult to appreciate the change in level between the Conigre and the area around Westcroft House. All that remains is the handrail of the Conigre Steps, now used as a railing outside Conigre Parsonage, but this picture of the steps gives some idea of the change in height. Two members of Trowbridge Camera Club, Mike Hayward and Roy Berrett, discuss their evening's photography.

THESE WERE PROBABLY SEVENTEENTH-CENTURY HOUSES, facing the open space in front of the Conigre Chapel, though with more recent windows and some mock timber-framing. Like a few other well-maintained houses in the Conigre, they were spared from the 1934 demolition and only disappeared when the whole area was changed in 1963.

LIKE OTHER LOCAL TOWNS, Trowbridge expanded in a period of flourishing trade after 1660 and a whole new area of housing appeared in the Conigre. By the nineteenth century it had become the poorest part of the town and most of it was demolished under a slum clearance scheme in 1934. At that time many of the seventeenth-century houses remained and it is a great pity that they were allowed to disappear unrecorded.

However, there are several photographs of the pump which stood in Lower Broad Street, and the mullioned windows and rubble stone walls in the background to this one are those of one of the original houses. The pump had been provided in 1844 and from it several water carriers took water round for sale.

THESE OLD HOUSES stood at the junction of the Conigre and Church Street and were typical of so much that has been lost in the interest of better traffic flow and wider streets – not architecturally distinguished, but so much more interesting than the brick wall which replaced them.

ALMOST ADJOINING THE LAST, where the entrance to Usher's British Row site is now, stood the old house of one branch of the Mortimer family. Built in the seventeenth century, as the blocked windows at the side show, it was refronted in the eighteenth and had at the back an extensive group of clothiers' workshops. It was demolished in 1969.

CONIGRE CHURCH SCHOOLROOM had been built right up to these houses that were being demolished in 1938. The dormer window in the larger house appears to be a later insertion of a weaver's window to allow enough light for a loom to be worked.

DEMOLITION at the back of The Harp, Shails Lane.

THE SOUTH SIDE OF LOWER BROAD STREET only consisted of these buildings after the great clearance of 1934. The two to the left were demolished to make way for the bus station, but the stone one (the lower part of the old Conigre Infants' School) survived until 1988, when it was demolished.

THIS LARGE HOUSE stood in Riverway (once called Gooseacre, then Gasworks Road) on the site now occupied by Ladds' car-park. Its frontage was eighteenth century, but the interior may have been older. It was called in its later days The Giffords (no reason for this name has been found) and early this century a dairy business was run from it.

SECTION FIVE

At Work and Travelling

In 1915 there were five woollen manufacturers in the town and times were prosperous with employment for townspeople and villagers. However when Kemp and Hewitt closed their Innox factory in 1954 the local industry was on its irrevocable decline. Fortunately other industries were to expand and new ones arrive to utilise the workforce. Bowyers and Usher's Wiltshire Brewery both grew considerably as did Chapmans (now Airspring) and after the war the site of the barracks was used for industrial development.

For much of this period transport for most people meant train, bus or bicycle. Train services were frequent with particularly good services to London in the inter-war years while both town and villages were well served by the bus companies. For many years it was mainly the 'gentry' and professional classes who owned motor cars although some enthusiasts were able to maintain vehicles with very little money. Motorbikes were popular, though sometimes unreliable, from the 1920s but it was not until the 1950s that car ownership became more commonplace.

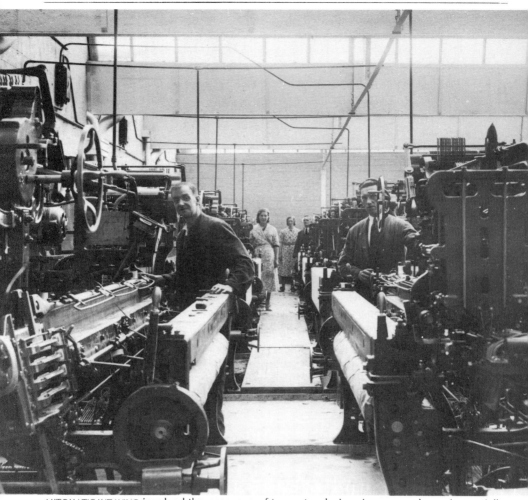

AUTOMATIC WEAVING involved the presence of two extra devices in a power loom (essentially, of course, an automatic machine anyway), one to change the bobbin in the shuttle as the supply of yarn ran out, the other to stop the loom if a warp thread broke. The purpose of both was to enable one weaver to look after more looms than hitherto and so save cost. Automatic looms with both features had been available for many years in 1937, but were not suitable for the types of cloth made in Trowbridge. Evidently McCalls, whose factory was on the site of today's Tesco, thought that a way forward was to fit looms of older type modified by adding the necessary mechanisms, and this is what is shown being done. These were the first automatics of any sort in Trowbridge; 36 were fitted in an additional shed and could be looked after by nine weavers. Another new feature was that each loom was driven by an electric motor, so that the pulleys and shafting still to be seen in other sheds were not needed.

UNTIL IT WAS DEMOLISHED IN 1967, Courts Mill formed part of one of the finest groups of historic textile buildings anywhere in the world, standing between the surviving parts – Courtfield House and Ashton Mill. The building nearer the camera was probably added around 1848; the projection with the long window was the beam engine house.

THE FIRST STEAM ENGINE in the whole local textile region was set up in Trowbridge in 1805 in an existing building, but the first factory built to be driven by steam from the start soon followed. It was Bridge Mill, built in 1808 near the Town Bridge; its site is now occupied by the Gateway Supermarket, empty at the time of writing. Bridge Mill was used to make cloth until 1897; it was then converted to a flour and provender mill by J.H. & S. Sainsbury. When they left in 1969 it was pulled down, so that the town had lost its two earliest and finest factory buildings in two years.

HOME MILL was built after a massive fire had destroyed the previous factory on the site in 1862, and was itself gutted by fire in 1931. About 250 hands were employed at the time. The firm, Samuel Salter & Co., was able to continue because the other manufacturers in the town worked up its orders. The factory was rebuilt, though minus its top storey, and continued at work until 1982.

SALTER'S MENDING SHOP in the 1920s. Mending involved repairing minor blemishes on the cloth. It was highly skilled, and quiet and clean compared with most jobs in the factory.

INNOX MILL stood on the Biss behind the houses of Innox Road. Its history of several centuries as a flour mill ended early in the present century and its last use was in connection with a scrap metal business. It was pulled down in the 1950s.

THE OTHER INNOX MILL is now the older part of Bowyers' factory adjoining the river. Until 1954 it was the cloth factory of Kemp & Hewitt. The date of this fire has not been found, but it was probably in the 1930s. The picture is looking towards the entrance from the Town Bridge; though now only a way through the factory, the lane, called Mill Lane, once led to the premises of several other firms further downstream.

The buildings in the background, once houses, were by this time part of the factory. They were destroyed by the 1942 bombing raid and replaced by the present flat-roofed building.

TROWBRIDGE STOCK MARKET was held on alternate Tuesdays in the 1930s and 40s when cattle, sheep and pigs were auctioned. Out of sight, to the left of this picture, were the coops and cages where the smaller livestock, geese, ducks, hens and rabbits, were held.

THE BATH & WEST SHOW was held at Hilperton on Mr Pike's land in 1937; here the showground is under construction showing the main pavilion. On Thursday 27 May it received a visit from the Duke of Kent. Also present was the Emperor of Abyssinia and the 30,067 people passing through the turnstiles in 4 days included 1,000 schoolchildren from the town and nearby villages. Wiltshire farmers were well represented and the greatest travellers were some sheep who had come from Australia to compete.

VERY FEW INNS AND PUBLIC HOUSES were still brewing their own beer. Howard John Langley had taken over The New Inn (now The Linnet) from his father, also the village bootmaker, in 1910. It had been owned by the Langley family since the 1830s. When pictured in November 1939 Mr Langley had ceased brewing a few years earlier although he still held a brewing licence. He did however still make cider, with local cider apples, or any fallers, brought to The New Inn to be pulped. The pulp was shovelled on to the press between layers of straw and a heavy wooden block placed on top. The layers would be squeezed in the press and the juice that ran out of the bottom was collected and stored in six hogsheads (each hogshead held 52½ gallons). After some months, or maybe a year, the cider was ready to drink.

THIS MASSIVE PIECE OF MACHINERY for Usher's bottling plant was brought into the town by Pickfords in 1937, pausing for the photographer outside Rodney House where it soon attracted a group of schoolchildren and errand boys.

On 23 November Mr T.C. Usher, Chairman of Usher's Wiltshire Brewery, set the new bottling plant in motion. It had been installed by the firm's engineers and would automatically fill bottles at the rate of two per minute. The opening was followed by a tour of the works and luncheon at the Roundstone Hotel.

In the year ending 30 September 1937 Ushers had filled 11,758, 548 bottles with their old equipment. This represented 33,442 barrels or 1,199,512 gallons of beer. The new bottling stores was now one of the most efficient in the country with beer kept in glass-lined conditioning tanks in the plant in Union Street.

1937 prices were: bitter and brown ale 6*d*. (2½p) a large bottle, home brewed, I.P.A. and oatmeal stout 7*d*. (3p) a large bottle.

THE OLD TROWBRIDGE CHRONICLE PRINT-ING WORKS in Narrow Wine Street were taken over by Frank Slugg & Co. who were general printers with customers over a wide area. In the 1950s the building faced the rear entrance of Woolworths and was a favourite area for local character Joe Collins as he cleaned the shopgirls' bicycles.

B. LANSDOWN & SON, who owned and printed *The Wiltshire Times*, were also general printers with their works in Duke Street. Until the mid-1930s their office and stationer's shop was at 6 Silver Street.

THAT MANY PEOPLE remained in employment with the same company is shown by this photograph from 23 September 1937. It marked the occasion when 85 employees with 25 years of service and over had a special presentation at the Nestlé factory at Staverton. The managing director of the company, Mr J.W. Gwynn, presented tankards to the men, clocks to the women and certificates to everyone. Staff from four Nestlé factories were present and among the long service workers were nearly 40 based at Staverton.

Ladies: Miss D. Bowyer, Miss F. Lane, Miss K. Lane, Miss E. Lansdown, Miss E.L.M. Osborne, Miss E.M. Pearce, Miss M.E. Purnell and Miss E.M. Taylor. Men: Mr H.G. Bainton, Mr F. Beaven, Mr H. Beaven, Mr A.J. Bennett, Mr W. Chapman, Mr F.W. Endru, Mr F.T. Fido, Mr H. Francis, Mr C. Gibbs, Mr H.H. Griffin, Mr G.F. Hale, Mr V.R. Hale, Mr A.E. Harrison, Mr F. Hutchings, Mr H. Lane, Mr R.S. Moore, Mr H.H.P. Perry, Mr E.W. Potter, Mr H.J. Price, Mr W.J. Pullen, Mr D.R. Sartain, Mr A.W. Stevens, Mr C.B. Stevens, Mr R.W. Taylor, Mr W.J. Taylor, Mr A. Vincent and Mr R.G. Wills.

A VERY SAD PICTURE in that it shows the vandalism that was visited upon this fine factory at Staverton. In March 1936 the former woollen mill, which had been rebuilt in 1824, suffered the indignity of having its top three storeys and the locally well-known Phoenix clock removed. At the same time a new factory block was built.

A GOOD GENERAL VIEW OF TROWBRIDGE RAILWAY STATION seen from the top of the tower of Holy Trinity Church, c. 1935. As well as noting some industrial buildings, now demolished, it is interesting to see the amount of rolling stock in the GWR station.

TROWRIDGE RAILWAY STATION was once a busy passenger junction and goods yard with three platforms, engine sheds, shunting engines and many sidings for goods trucks. This picture from 1938 shows some of the complexity of the lines. The original station had been built to a Brunel design in stone and during the 1950s the staff often won awards for the best kept station in the area.

On this occasion, Monday 11 April 1938, twenty conditioning tanks had been brought from Scotland for Usher's Wiltshire Brewery. It was believed to be the largest single delivery of tanks ever made in England at that time. The tanks cost £4,000 and held 30,000 gallons.

LOWER STUDLEY (now Dursley Road and Drynham) was until 1870 largely a cottage settlement, still semi-rural. About then several terraces were built on the west side of Dursley Road; the occupiers of them found that their quickest way to town was to cross the railway and join the footpath which led from the stone bridge near the present Dursley Arms down to Cradle Bridge. A footbridge to enable them to cross safely was erected in 1886. The field across the line is now occupied by Cherry Gardens. In the background can be seen Home Close Farm and the two houses which stood near the clap-gate at the point where the footpath left the road to the farm.

WHEN TURNPIKE TRUSTS WERE SET UP round Trowbridge in the middle of the eighteenth century, a main road from Bath to Salisbury passed through the town and out by Green Lane to Steeple Ashton. A turnpike gate stood where Polebarn Lane crossed the Paxcroft Brook and entered what was, until 1818, Ashton Common. The first gatekeeper's house stood on the west side of the road, but it was replaced c. 1840 by a larger one opposite, shown in this photograph. It remained in use as a private house until it was demolished in the 1960s.

BEFORE THE ADVENT OF PUBLIC TRANSPORT it was the carriers who transported people and their belongings from railway station, market or shop to villages and outlying areas. Frank Chivers of Dilton Marsh, pictured outside Rodney House in 1939, was the last carrier in business in Trowbridge.

THE MOTOR CAR QUICKLY SPREAD to all parts of Trowbridge. In the 1920s this large-bodied sedan was to be found in the Conigre.

THE COUNCIL FOR THE PRESERVATION OF RURAL ENGLAND ran a competition in Wiltshire in 1937 aimed at improving the appearance of petrol stations in the county. The proliferation of unsightly petrol stations in previously unspoilt villages had been causing concern in much of the country during the 1930s. There were 46 entries in four classes and the winner of the class for a petrol station in a rural area with three pumps or less was the Southwick Filling Station of A.E. Holloway. Besides offering petrol from 1s. 4d. (6½p) a gallon and oil from 1s. (5p) a quart, the Southwick Station provided refreshment for travellers and would also hire a car to those unfortunates who were without one or had suffered a breakdown with their own.

FORE STREET GARAGES (KNEES) were main dealers for Hillman cars. In 1938 the Hillman Minx Safety Saloon was priced at £169 with tax of £7 10s. 0d. (£7.50). By buying on hire purchase you could drive one away for £42 5s. 0d. (£42.25). In 1939 the Hillman Hawk Safety Saloon, with Triplex glass windows, cost £295 at the upper end of the range. New cars that had been used as demonstrators ranged in price from £100 to £235.

STONEY GUTTER CROSSROADS seems to have become an accident black spot shortly after the invention of the internal combustion engine! In the 1930s there were a spate of mishaps and on 17 April 1937 the Ford car, on the left, was in collision with the Austin and came to rest within inches of dropping into a small stream.

THE CHILDREN'S CARNIVAL and the fair took over much of the park in the 1950s. In the Lower Park and Court Fields were the large 'rides', boxing booths and many side shows while the Upper Park contained children's roundabouts and candy floss and toffee apple stalls. This traction engine has strayed to the top of the park where it has drawn an admiring crowd.

THIS AEROPLANE, from the Royal Flying School at Yatesbury, crash landed in a field at Semington on 1 April 1938. *The Wiltshire Times* published this picture on 2 April claiming it as an 'exclusive' and stating that the aeroplane was piloted by a young man named Hearst. Presumably he escaped unhurt as that is all the paper said about the incident. During World War II the presence of aircraft made itself known in the area with 'shadow factories' in Trowbridge where many local people, mostly beyond military age, did their bit for the war effort making aircraft components.

SECTION SIX

Councils and Public Service

Most of the functions of the present District Council were carried out by the Urban District Council and the Rural District Councils. After the establishment of Wiltshire County Council in 1889 many of its meetings were held in Trowbridge as it was the easiest town to reach by rail from all other parts of the county. The Town Hall was originally intended to provide a meeting place for the Council, but various other buildings were leased or later built. The effects of housing the County Offices have been considerable although they were probably less noticeable in the period up to 1959.

Trowbridge Hospital, in The Halve, (the present one was built in 1929) had been given to the town in 1886 by Mrs Gouldsmith who also presented the soup kitchen in Frog Lane. The town had a cemetery from 1856, a market hall from 1862, a piped water supply from 1874, sewage disposal from 1895 and had enjoyed gas street lights before Bath. A range of schools in town and village fulfilled the demands of the Education Act with secondary education concentrated in Trowbridge; from 1891 a Textile School had provided instruction in the staple industry.

AT THE GENERAL ELECTION OF 1950 the crowds still gathered in front of the Town Hall to hear the result of voting in the Westbury Division, announced from the balcony at about midday on the Friday following Thursday's polling. The crowd was not deterred by rain, nor was Mr Robert Grimston, returned as Conservative MP for the constituency for the fourth time, as he walked bare-headed, with police escort, to give the traditional short speech to Conservative supporters from an upper window of The George Hotel. Mr Grimston was later knighted and on his retirement from the House of Commons was made an hereditary peer as Baron Grimston of Westbury.

ALL MEETINGS OF THE COUNTY COUNCIL from 1899 have been held in Trowbridge and after various premises had been leased the County Offices, in Hill Street, were built in 1913. By 1929 this was too small to accommodate the numbers of staff and in 1930 the Council voted in favour of building new offices in Devizes. After an economic crisis and some fierce controversy the decision was changed in favour of Trowbridge in 1933. The site of the Trowbridge Town football ground was acquired in 1937 and the contract awarded to Messers J. Long & Son of Bath at a cost of £150,000. Built to a design of P.D. Hepworth, the lower picture shows the building that arose on the empty site above, where the mechanical excavator is stuck in the mud.

THE CONTRACT FOR 134 DWELLINGS to rehouse the inhabitants of the Conigre was awarded in November 1934; the cost was £39,101. When this opening ceremony was performed by Mr G. Shakespeare MP, 116 houses had been roofed by 12 July 1935. The total number of houses and bungalows to be built had risen to 154 on the 12 acre site. Altogether over 2.3 million bricks and over 100,000 tiles were used. All bricks used in external walls were made in Trowbridge at the yard of Mr A.S. Crees in Wyke Road.

After the opening the 'Great Trek' began with wheel-barrows, hand-carts, go-carts and prams piled high with possessions pushed up the hill from Conigre to the new houses. The people were leaving behind conditions such as a family of twelve in one house, one lavatory shared between three families and a family of eight with only two bedrooms.

The Wiltshire Times commented that the new estate 'may not be a thing of beauty but undoubtedly it will be a joy for ever'. Quite true, but although the families from the slums most definitely had to be rehoused one fervently wishes that the old houses had been left for restoration.

The name of the new estate in 1935 was the old field name of Gooseacre; it would have been pleasant had this name remained in use.

THE PEOPLE'S PARK viewed from the Town Hall in the early 1920s. The young Cornish elms were planted as memorials to the Trowbridge men who fell in the Great War. Prominent to the left are the factories of Palmer & MacKay's Courts Mill.

THE SECOND URBAN DISTRICT COUNCIL HOUSING SCHEME was at Lower Studley Fields, now Longfield. The contractor, Mr E.J.G. Morgan of Uxbridge, began work on 1 August 1936 and when this picture was taken on 8 September 34 dwellings were up to window-sill height. Altogether 124 houses, including 12 bungalows, were planned for the site.

THE TROWBRIDGE LIBRARY was, until 1959, housed in a decayed Presbyterian Chapel, built c. 1703, with the public area on the ground floor. When the library moved to the Old County Offices in Hill Street membership rose by 55 per cent. The chapel was demolished in 1961 to make way for the Silver Street Co-operative store.

PUPILS AT ADCROFT SCHOOL constructed this pond in the school grounds in 1934 and were then able to add nature study to their curriculum.

THE TROWBRIDGE DIVISION OF THE WILTSHIRE POLICE pictured on 14 April 1930 on the occasion of the retirement of Superintendent Underwood. Back row: P.C. Pye, P.C. Webb, P.C. Blake, P.C. Betteridge, P.C. Chivers, P.C. Selley, P.C. Kemp. Fourth row: P.C. Matthews, P.C. Sutton, P.C. Butcher, P.C. Frankcom, P.C. Stanley, P.C. Bunce, P.C. Shaw. Third row: P.C. Grant, P.C. Claydon, P.C. Gosling, P.C. Rowden, P.C. Pearce, P.C. Payne, P.C. Griffin, P.C. Gape. Second row: P.S. Stokes, P.S. Mackie, Inspector Ferris, Superintendent Underwood, Inspector Coleman, P.S. Waylen, P.C. Mathews. Seated on ground: P.C. Poole, P.C. Sanday, P.C. Midgley, P.C. King.

THE SEMINGTON POOR LAW INSTITUTION, or Workhouse as it was universally known, was built in 1835 to hold 35 'inmates'. It had become more humanitarian by the 1920s when the Trowbridge, Melksham and Bradford Guardians were pictured with the staff on the occasion of an entertainment for the inhabitants. Back row: H. Davis, T.A. Talbott, W.J. Dowty, J.H. Hatcher, E. Belcher, F.J. Rogers, T. Cole, Mrs Cole, F. Barnett, R.H. Rodway. Third row: A. Knight, A.M. Pike, E.J. Lee, J. Cripps, W.H.E. Greenhill, P.E.T. Garrett, W.B. Norris, R. Morgan-Smith, A.H. Moore, Miss Williams, Mrs R.H. Hudson, A.J. Woodward. Second row: Dr Bennett, Sister Woodward, Miss F. Denny, Nurse Golding, Nurse Bishop, Mrs Hatcher, W. Hayter, Mrs Taylor, C.H. Taylor, Revd Jackson, Mrs Paynter, Nurse Ryland, Nurse Caley. Front row: Mrs Doel, Mrs Knee, F.H. Knee, Mrs Pullinger, Miss Godwin, J.H. Bishop, Miss E.F. Mann, G. Stratton, Miss Wheeler, W.J. Stokes, Mrs Millard, Mrs Ball.

ADCROFT SCHOOL became the LCC Hammersmith School in the early 1940s. It provided a three-year course of practical education for children aged 13 to 14½ years and began with 70 pupils, mainly from the London area. As well as a general education such subjects as building construction, plumbing, surveying, heating and ventilating, and commercial art were taught.

ONE OF THE LAST TIMES THAT TROWBRIDGE SOUP KITCHEN OPENED ITS DOORS to the poor and needy was 1936. Venison, from Bellefield House, was supplied and a bewildering variety of jugs was brought to carry home the nourishing soup.

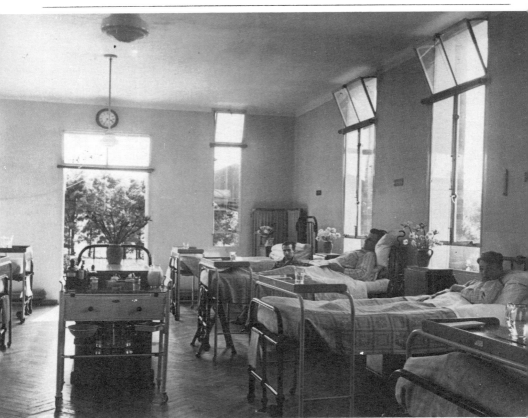

PATIENTS AT TROWBRIDGE AND DISTRICT HOSPITAL in the new men's ward that was opened in August 1937.

Below right:
Saturday 24 March 1934 saw the opening of the new youth hostel at Steeple Ashton near The Long's Arms. It replaced one at South Down Farm, Bratton, which had recently been included in the military zone. The new hostel lay at the rear of the house of Mr and Mrs Whiting, the wardens, and utilised the buildings of the former Rood Ashton estate yard. Accommodation was 1s. (5p) a night.

THE OLD CLINIC IN THE HALVE, which was replaced by the present building in 1964 occupied a building which was opened in 1883 as the town's first purpose-built Cottage Hospital. The hospital had been started in 1870 in Fernleigh House, Church Street, now the office of a firm of accountants. When the new Trowbridge and District Hospital was opened in the adapted and extended Adcroft House in 1929 the old building was adapted for use as the County Council Clinic.

THE DATE OF THIS PICTURE IS NOT KNOWN, but it probably dates from just before or during the war. The firemen are handling an auxiliary pump of the type which could be quickly towed to an outbreak of fire caused by bombing.

COUNTY HALL was damaged by a fire which destroyed the roof at the Drill Hall and the clock tower in January 1958. Many stored medical records were also destroyed.

TROWBRIDGE HAD ONLY GAS LAMPS IN THE STREETS until 1950 and had the reputation of being the worst-lit town in the country. Then the centre was fitted with white fluorescent electric lights, although gas survived much longer in some other streets. By 1950 the lamplighter and his pole were a thing of the past, and the gas lamps were fitted with clocks. Going round to wind about 400 of them weekly was a big job and Bill Beak of Harmony Place, cycling slowly along with his ladder precariously balanced on his shoulder, was a well-known figure, both in his job and as a Labour member of the town council. Here he is winding the clock on the lamp in the centre of the road in front of the Town Hall.

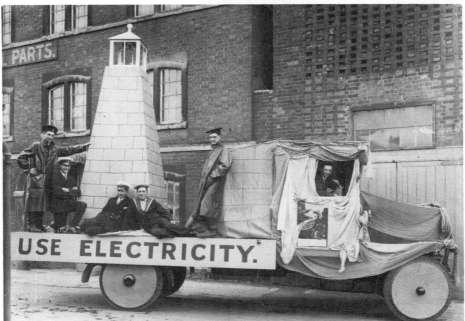

THIS TABLEAU must have been prepared, no doubt for Trowbridge Carnival, by the West Wilts Light & Power Co. Ltd., probably c. 1930. At that time it supplied power to an area stretching to Chippenham, Devizes and Westbury. The picture was taken in front of Castle Factory, Court Street, and shows the now-vanished handle house which adjoined it.

FOR MANY YEARS a tall iron gas lamp standard stood outside the Town Hall. By the mid-1950s it was deemed that there was sufficient illumination in the area without this standard awkwardly placed in the middle of a busy road junction. Its demolition required the use of pneumatic drills as it was very firmly set in a large block of concrete.

THE OCCASION OF THIS PICTURE IS UNKNOWN, but in the 1920s this telegraph pole must have carried more lines than any other in Trowbridge and the engineers were proud to pose on it.

A GREAT THUNDERSTORM on 25 June 1935 between 3.00 p.m. and 4.30 p.m. caused much damage in western Wiltshire and was recorded as being the worst in living memory. There was no loss of human life, but several narrow escapes and many animals and poultry were drowned. The River Avon rose quickly and caused this extensive flooding at Staverton.

TROWBRIDGE HAD RECEIVED ITS WATER SUPPLY FROM UPTON SCUDAMORE since the 1870s. In 1934 a new borehole was sunk which provided 34,000 gallons of sand-free water per hour for use by the towns of Trowbridge and Melksham.

FLOODWATER had damaged the river bridge at Blackball Hatches thereby cutting short a favourite walk of Trowbridgians from the south-eastern part of the town. In 1939, through the kindness of a town councillor and the permission of local farmer Mr T.C. Corp, this footbridge was erected. For local people, unable to afford a summer holiday, the common answer to the question 'Where are you going on holiday this year?' was 'Blackball Hatches'.

THE PEOPLE'S DISPENSARY FOR SICK ANIMALS OF THE POOR visited Trowbridge in August 1935. Miss Copland-Griffiths had done great work in founding a service in the Bath and Wiltshire district and it was hoped to raise money for a permanent caravan service.

Celebrations, Entertainment and the Sporting Life

National events such as jubilees and coronations were enthusiastically celebrated with streets, shops and buildings decorated in patriotic colours. Local events included the Trowbridge & District Hospital Carnival, flower shows, large fêtes and garden parties. Much of the entertainment was home grown and amateur although a surprising number of professional entertainers did come to the area. Both the circus and the fair were eagerly awaited visitors to the Lower Park and Court Fields. The first purpose-built Trowbridge cinema opened in 1913 and by the late 1930s there were three, two of which had seating for a thousand or more. Many organisations held dinners and dances, mainly in The George, and hosted parties for children.

Trowbridge Town Football Club had successful teams throughout this period while each village was able to field at least one football and cricket team. The County Ground was established at the top of Timbrell Street for cricket and athletics and provided a home for Trowbridge Cricket Club. Rugby was played and many sports and pastimes were centred upon the pubs, darts, skittles and cribbage all having their own leagues.

SEVEN-YEAR-OLD STANLEY HICKERTON poses with his coronation mug and souvenir booklet in Upper Alma Street on the occasion of the coronation of King George VI in 1937.

FOR THE JUBILEE CELEBRATIONS OF 1935 the Trowbridge group of scouts built a 20 ft. high beacon at Clarendon which was lit at 10.00 p.m. and burned all night. During the day a representative 12 scouts, under Scoutmaster A.A. Pinker, marched in the procession that is pictured at the bottom of Hilperton Road.

THE JUBILEE OF KING GEORGE V in May 1935 was celebrated in many ways in Trowbridge. There were half a crown (12½p) vouchers for old age pensioners, the unemployed over 18 years and the sick and needy. Children, aged between 5 and 15 received a jubilee book that was otherwise on sale at one shilling (5p). At the Palace Cinema tableaux representing the Empire were staged, Miss Cynthia Stancomb sang, the White-Massey Dancing School performed and the British Legion Band played. A well-attended Jubilee Dance was held at the Town Hall, the whole front of The George was decorated by its hosts Mr and Mrs Chinn while all the town looked festive and gay. In the park 1,600 children joined together to enjoy various entertainments including a display of dancing by pupils of Mrs L.A. Thomas and Miss P. Thomas. They then all sang 'God Save the King' and marched off to their various churches and chapels to have tea.

AFTER THE CRISIS over the abdication of King Edward VIII it must have been something of a relief to be able to proclaim the Duke of York as King George VI from the Town Hall steps in December 1936.

THE CORONATION OF HER MAJESTY QUEEN ELIZABETH II saw what was probably the first widespread use of street parties in Trowbridge. In residential streets where there was little or no through traffic, trestle tables were erected and chairs brought out from each house. Several days had been spent in baking and the preparation of trifles, jellies and blancmanges – all from ingredients that had but lately been rationed. A wide variety of crockery showed the tastes of individual households but none of that bothered the children who, having their own coronation mugs, were eagerly awaiting the feast.

This scene was in Upper Alma Street, where children from several surrounding streets had congregated. The photograph, taken by Charles Marshman, was selected for an album presented by the Photographic Dealers Association to the Queen in commemoration of her coronation on 2 June 1953.

MEMBERS AND OFFICERS OF THE TROWBRIDGE URBAN DISTRICT COUNCIL assembled on the Town Hall steps (left) as the chairman, Mr Percy Inglis, reads the proclamation of the accession to the throne of Queen Elizabeth II. Among the platform party are Canon R.L. Pelly, Miss Maude Moser, Mr George Applegate senior, Mr Denis Mugford, Mr Ieuan Evans, Mr H. Holloway and Mr Les Miles. The press photographer on the right is Reggie Highfield of the *Bath Chronicle* and the *Wiltshire News*.

THE LIBERAL FÊTE at the Flower Show Field (now the Stallards Recreation Field) was an eagerly awaited social event. In July 1937 this gathering was addressed by Richard Acland, the Liberal MP for Barnstaple. Harold Dewey, the chairman of the local Association Executive, in his speech urged the need for an electoral system of proportional representation.

On this occasion the fête was one of the most successful seen for many years with, among the entertainers, top of the bill cabaret act Rupert Hazell and Elsie Day. Also appearing were the Moxham Trio of trick cyclists and singers Hilda Bickham and George Taylor, while the Steeple Ashton Band played during the afternoon. The tug of war winners were a team from Bowyers, Messers Studts Fun Fair was enjoyed by old and young alike and in the evening there was a firework display.

In the background of this picture can be seen the railway station sidings and goods wagons.

THE CO-OPERATIVE DAY OF THE TROWBRIDGE SOCIETY, Saturday 5 July 1930, was a beautiful day, intensely hot. Sports for 800 children of members were held at the Flower Show Field, followed by a procession to the Society's offices at Rodney House headed by the Steeple Ashton Band. There the children were given tea and each was presented with a rubber ball. At this time the Trowbridge Co-operative Society had just over 7,000 members. In 1930 they spent £194,968 in the shops in Trowbridge, Melksham and Westbury, for which they received a 'divi' of 1s. 3d. (7½p) in the pound. Trowbridge remained an independent Society until 1966, when it became part of the Bath & West Co-operative Society. This picture was taken in the grounds of Rodney House. The Society's president, Hubert Long, is the tall man without a hat, right centre.

THE OPEN-AIR FÊTES of the local Conservative and Liberal constituency parties were always on a grand scale and involved many months of preparation. This group is from the West Wilts Liberal Fête, c. 1920, with the be-suited gent, McWilliam Phipp, in the centre with his daughter, Peggy, in front of him.

CHILDREN'S PARTIES with local entertainers were very popular and were often staged by areas, such as Lower Studley, that had a good community spirit and a 'togetherness'. On Thursday 6 January 1938 these children of Lower Studley gathered in the Co-operative Hall for tea, games and songs.

THE REGAL CINEMA, in Bythesea Road, was opened on Monday 1 November 1937 by Mr F.P. Garlick, chairman of Trowbridge Town Council, seen with Mr C. Ingham Haden, president of Trowbridge Hospital, Mr B.J. Vale, managing director, Mr Wright, director, and the manager, Mr Stanley W. Banks, whose slogan was 'We are at your service'.

Below is the interior of the cinema which had seating for a thousand people, a heating and ventilating system that could pump out 750,000 cubic feet of fresh air per hour and a telephone number of 'Trowbridge 1'. The opening performance was the comedy, *Feather Your Nest*, featuring George Formby, and the takings of £20 were given to the hospital.

A LITTLE LATER, on Monday 29 November, the New Gaumont opened on the site of the old Palace Cinema in Fore Street. This had 1,250 seats, the Palace had only 650, and was fully air-conditioned. As their rivals at the Regal had beaten them in opening a new cinema the Gaumont-British Film Studio brought in the Countess of Radnor to perform the ceremony and the young British star, Margaret Lockwood, to attract the paying public.

There was not a vacant seat on the first night and the audience enjoyed Paul Robeson in *King Solomon's Mines* and a comedy called, *Oh Doctor!* During the second half of the week the feature film was *Lloyds of London* with the boy film star from Warminster, Freddie Bartholomew.

Lady Radnor and Margaret Lockwood had taken tea at The George before crossing the road to the cinema where they were presented with bouquets of chrysanthemums by Hazel Bigwood, daughter of the cinema manager, Mr G.F. Bigwood.

CONCERTS AND CONCERT PARTIES were very popular in the inter-war years and there was much local amateur talent. This group of young people performed at Staverton on the evenings of 19 and 20 December in 1919.

THE 1938 PRODUCTION FROM THE TROWBRIDGE OPERATIC SOCIETY was *The Belle of New York*, at the Town Hall, which included this bevy of bridesmaids. It was considered their best ever effort in the 16 years since they had opened with *The Gondoliers* in 1922. Music was provided by a full orchestra.

THE OLD PARK BANDSTAND (above) was replaced in 1939 by the one (below) given by Mr W. Nelson Haden. The opening took place at 2.45 p.m. on 22 July 1939 and the first band to perform, that evening, was the band of HM Royal Artillery, Portsmouth. It was said to be one of the best bandstands in the West Country.

THE YOUNG LADIES of Miss White's and Miss Massey's Dancing School on their 1927 carnival float that was mounted on a farm cart. Pictured on the Flower Show Field with Trinity Church in the background.

A GREAT BRITISH SHIP, *The Queen Mary*, is recalled by this 1934 carnival entry 'Cunarder 534' which was the name given to the vessel before her launch. Winning prizes in both Trowbridge and Frome Carnivals the ship was mounted on a pram and would emit smoke from her funnels.

THIS CO-OPERATIVE SOCIETY TRADE FLOAT of 1935 was the first carnival entry to be fully illuminated by electricity. Built by Alec Hickerton and Jack Hill it used car batteries as its source of power and, as well as taking part in local carnivals, the well-lit float caused a surprise in local villages on evening visits.

CARNIVAL ENTRIES required preparation at evenings and weekends for several weeks by 1935. This monster was built by the young men from the printers, Frank Slugg. Ron Harding and Charles Marshman are to the right of the group.

CARNIVAL ENTRIES for the Grand Procession in the 1950s assembled and were judged at the barracks in Frome Road, from where they set out on their circuit around the town. The above picture shows a military band moving off from the entrance to the barracks; the Victorian block is on the left and the cavalry buildings of 1794 in the background. Below is a float portraying the England and Australia Test Match series travelling towards the junction with Bradley Road. The now demolished stone curtain wall of the barracks is in the background.

THE RAISED GROUNDS OF THE WESLEY ROAD CHAPEL was a favourite vantage point during the carnival processions of the 1950s. A tableau representing the Fountain of Youth, a favourite theme involving the use of young ladies, passes Newtown School and its gardens that were created from derelict allotments in 1938.

A TOUCH OF THE EXOTIC was essential in a fair of the 1950s even if the Cuban dancing girls had never been beyond the shores of Europe. The job of the barker, on the right, was to hint at many more delights than were available for the 1s. (5p) admission money.

THE FUNFAIR associated with Trowbridge Carnival was often held in the Market Yard in the 1920s. In the foreground, near the sheep pens, stand the traction engines which provided the power to the fairground rides and carousels.

In a small town like Trowbridge the fair provided an opportunity for boisterous behaviour and a general letting off of steam; behaviour that would not have been tolerated elsewhere but which could use the fair as a safety valve. Besides the roundabouts, Noah's ark, swing boats and helter-skelter there were many side shows, coconut shies, rifle ranges and exhibitions of strange beings, both animal and human.

PART OF CHIPPERFIELD'S CIRCUS reached Trowbridge by train around 1955. The eleven elephants disembarked at the railway station and made their way along Bythesea Road into Mortimer Street before reaching their temporary home in the park. The occasion provided excellent publicity for the circus and a free show for the townspeople.

WATCHING THE ERECTION OF THE BIG TOP, c. 1955, provided plenty of opportunity to anticipate the thrills that were in store for anyone making an evening visit to the circus.

THE PARK was always a source of entertainment for the young. Here impromptu games of football and cricket took place while the slide, erected in 1936, and the swings provided excitement for the children and some slight anxiety for their mothers. Safer, apart from splinters, was the roundabout, pictured in 1951.

DANCING IN THE STREETS was not a normal spectacle in the 1950s, but a group of morris dancers have stopped the traffic outside the Town Hall and persuaded Trowbridgians to join them.

ROOD ASHTON PARK had for long been one of the amenities of the Trowbridge area. Between the wars local people would take walks through the park and around its lake and in the late 1950s, November 5th was celebrated with large bonfires. During World War II the area had reverted to pastureland and in the 1950s the Hall was stripped and became derelict. In the mid-1950s a large boy scout jamboree took place here with many local troops participating.

TROWBRIDGE CYCLING CLUB was a dedicated band of enthusiasts who organised many events including time trials. A complementary group, of cyclists and campers, were the Trowbridge Wheelers. In 1937 typical day outings included one to Weston-super-Mare and back via Cheddar Gorge, a total of 90 miles, and trip to Southampton starting from Gloucester Road Post Office at 7.30 a.m.

A.G. STREET, at the back, the well-known Wiltshire writer, broadcaster and farmer, took part in an outside broadcast from Trowbridge, c. 1937. Also in the picture are Charles Lansdown, editor of *The Wiltshire Times*, (far left), the Rector, the Revd Nisbet Wallace, Sam Hector, bellringer and landlord of The White Swan, (second right) and Colin Lawson (far right) who was later to work for the *Daily Express*.

THE BRITISH LEGION BOYS BUGLE BAND were resplendent in their bright red tunics and navy blue trousers in February 1941. The band had been recently formed by its bandmaster, Mr F. Connor, and secretary, Mr R.G. Sutton and money for instruments and uniforms was raised by public subscription.

THE CUP WINNING FOOTBALL TEAM of Adcroft School in 1935 was supported by their well-known headmaster, Mr Bingham, on the left of the picture.

THESE TEAMS played in a match at the County Ground on 25 June 1931 to mark the 50th year that Fred Stancomb had been captain of Trowbridge Cricket Club, a record thought then to be unique. He also had the unusual distinction of having captained Wiltshire for some years at both cricket and football, playing full back for Trowbridge Town for a number of seasons. Col. R.W. Awdry, who captained the other team in the celebration match, said that he had played cricket with Fred Stancomb for 35 years and never seen him ruffled or heard him complain about a decision.

The picture shows, left to right, back row: J. Francis, W.H. Payne, C.N. Vaisey, F.S. Clark, G.F. Snailum, S.E. Hewitt, C.N. W. Blair, C. Murray Shireff. Centre row: G.K. Mattock, E.P. Awdry, W. Lovell Hewitt, S.L. Amor, G.A. Laverton, K. Smith, A.A. Batley, A.H. Bezer. Front row: C.W. Hurn, F.H. Moore, J. Mackie, F.W. Stancomb, R.W. Awdry, W.R. Campbell Laverton, A.G. Hurn, T.A. Pitts. In front: D.R. Lloyd, A.H. Dunn.

STEEPLE ASHTON FC beat Melksham St Andrews on Saturday 27 April 1935, at Trowbridge Town's ground, in the Trowbridge Knock Out Cup Final to win the new cup presented by Mr and Mrs F.W. Stancomb. At this time Steeple Ashton played in Division 2 of the Trowbridge League and finished in fourth position in the 1934/35 season.

ONE OF THE FINAL GAMES that Trowbridge Town FC played at their Bythesea Road ground before the site was developed for County Hall, c. 1937.

MANY THOUSANDS HAVE FOLLOWED THE FORTUNES OF TROWBRIDGE TOWN FOOTBALL CLUB over the 100 years of their history. Their greatest successes probably came either side of World War II with some famous FA Cup matches. In 1938 they won the Wiltshire Cup in a replayed final at Spencer Moulton's ground at Bradford-on-Avon. In the first match at Devizes the score had been Trowbridge 3: 1st Survey Co. (Royal Artillery, Larkhill) 3. In the very sportsmanlike replay the Town ran out winners by 3 goals to 0 with Hunt, Allen (own goal) and Powell all scoring in the first half. The Trowbridge team, led by their popular captain Billy Keates, were: goalkeeper, Whatley; full backs, Gunstone and Harding; half backs, Sullivan, Miles and Hansford; forwards, Keates, Powell, Prentice, Brabbam and Hunt.

AFTER THEIR EVICTION from Bythesea Road, Trowbridge Town Football Club moved to their present ground at Frome Road. They took with them their wooden grandstand, now unfortunately burned down, but in 1939 the Supporters Club decided to build another covered stand where spectators could keep dry free of charge. It was built by about ten members of the committee, using all their spare time, so as to have it completed for the opening of the 1939/40 season. It measured 60ft. by 18ft. and still stands today, though in a slightly dilapidated condition.

THE COUNTY CRICKET GROUND had a variety of uses including being the venue for the Wiltshire County School Sports. On 22 June 1935 Colonel R.W. Awdry is taking the Olympic salute at this rather militaristic march past. In the background is the area now covered by the houses of the Seymour Road estate.

TROWBRIDGE SWIMMING POOL was opened on Saturday 13 May, having first been proposed in 1919 and eventually costing £8,000 to build. The ceremony was performed by Mr W.G. Excott, president of the Wiltshire Amateur Swimming Association, watched by more than a thousand people. It was followed by a swimming gala which contained this mixed relay race.

THIS SCENE WAS CAPTURED on 7 June during a hot spell when the fountain had been temporarily switched off. In just over three weeks since the pool had been opened thousands of people had taken to the water and £150 taken in admission money.

FOR CENTURIES The George had been a focal point of life in Trowbridge. In the 1930s the hunt still met there and immobilised any traffic by a great concourse of hounds, horses and spectators. The number of bicycles perhaps indicates that some townsmen would be following the hunt on two wheels while others would be on foot trying to keep the hounds in sight.

Shops and Local People

Being a market town Trowbridge attracted shoppers from a large rural area. Although villages would have their post office, general store and perhaps one or two other shops the bulk of a household's purchases were made in the town. Meat and fish were most frequently bought in the town rather than elsewhere and of course that was where the more specialised shops were to be found. The Co-operative Society was an important influence in the town with several shops, while both Knees and Fear Hills had large departmental stores.

It is likely that photographs still exist of most of the people who have lived in the area during the twentieth century. Of these just a few of the ordinary inhabitants have been included, not the important figures but a cross section of the people who lived, loved and laughed, worked and experienced tragedy or sorrow within our community.

THE FINE VICTORIAN PREMISES now used by the Ramsbury Building Society were originally put up for Bowyers' retail shop in 1894, but a few years later they were sold to Albert Crook, a fishmonger. For many years the building was divided into two shops: when this picture was taken in the 1920s they were occupied by Whartons, fish and poultry dealers, and Pikes, confectioners.

AN ALMOST FORGOTTEN TROWBRIDGE INDUSTRY was the manufacture of brushes, which was carried on by Avons & Sons in a former cloth factory in Court Street. They made an amazing variety of brushes, from large industrial roller brushes to tooth brushes. Their retail shop, an ancient building, was replaced in 1928 by that now occupied by Mr Minit.

THE NEW CO-OPERATIVE STORES was opened in Mortimer Street in June 1936 (to the south of The Greyhound). Much of the goods stacked in tins and packets was from the Co-operative Wholesale Society with a prominent display of CWS biscuits in the foreground. The building's architect was Mr T. Snailum and the contractor was Mr A.W. Stow of Southwick.

MR HAMATON took delivery of his new Austin van on 30 June 1937. Hamatons Stores Ltd., of Silver Street, was then able to offer a speedy delivery service to its customers in outlying areas.

SILVER STREET, looking east, probably in the 1920s when Fear Hills still occupied premises on both sides of the street, and the house and shops occupied by Hiltons Boots and Shoes still had its original brick and stone Georgian front. This latter was replaced by the present Pitman House facade in 1939 for Wilkins & Darking and the Trowbridge Music Saloon (W.H. Benjamin, later R.A. Graham).

SILVER STREET, looking west, some time after 1937, when Ashplant's shoe shop took the former *Wiltshire Times*' newsagents premises (now S.K. Fruits) and Fear Hills had given up the premises now occupied by the TSB and the Leeds Building Society. Neither picture shows the front of the New Inn, demolished in the 1960s to make way for the Co-operative department store.

GENTLEMEN'S OUTFITTERS WILKINS & CO. held a sale before their compulsory removal from number 2 to number 10 Silver Street.

WILKINS & CO. had become Wilkins & Darking at 10 Silver Street by 1938 and we see Pitman House in its pre-1939 state. In that year the façade was re-modelled to its present appearance and both Wilkins & Darking and Benjamin continued to trade there until very recent times.

SUITS MADE TO MEASURE for 25s. (£1.25) seems cheap but in the 1930s it was about half the average weekly wage. The Red Lion, in Fore Street, survived until 1956 when it was taken over by Currys.

A SECTION OF THE LOWER PART OF FORE STREET in the 1950s. Liptons is now occupied by The Trowbridge Bookshop and the jewellers is now Chillcotts. Boots moved to their larger purpose-built shop higher up the street in the 1960s.

ANOTHER OF THE COMMERCIAL BUILDINGS OF 1865, in the same style and by the same builder as the Roundstone Hotel, which has survived intact above the ground floor. However, it lost its distinctive arcaded shop-front in 1935, when the present shop-front and facia were installed for H.J. Knee Ltd.'s ironmongery department, later the electrical department. The facia was a mottled warm grey marble and the lettering bright yellow.

The big department store founded by Henry J. Knee in 1879 in an old building on the site of Foster Bros. present shop, and transferred to a grand new building at the corner of Castle Street in 1887, is still family owned and managed and playing a leading role in the importance of Trowbridge as a shopping centre. It is now concentrated in the buildings beyond Red Hat Lane and its former premises in Fore Street, including this shop, are now occupied by several separate 'multiples'.

THE VISIT OF BERTRAM MILLS' CIRCUS in May 1936 provided shop manager Albert Taylor with the opportunity for good publicity for Foster Brothers. He produced trousers for both the circus dwarf and the 'giant' although fitting out the latter would have been rather more expensive than the 30s. (£1.50) being charged for ready-made suits. Boys' regulation grey flannel suits were 11s. 11d. (60p).

THE INTERNATIONAL STORES were built at the corner of Fore Street and Market Street in the 1930s. The picture shows excavations for the foundations with a lorry having reversed a little too far.

AT THE CORNER OF DUKE STREET AND CHURCH STREET, Rogers' ironmongery and kitchen-ware shop occupied one of the oldest buildings in the town dating, in part, probably from the original development of Duke Street in the 1690s, but so much altered and extended in later centuries that it became a fascinating jumble of styles and features. Closed in the 1980s it lay derelict for some years until its partial demolition and careful restoration began in 1988.

THESE TWO PHOTOGRAPHS show an interesting contrast in shop provision. Above, pictured in 1934, are purpose-built shops and flats in Frome Road. Planned to serve an expanding community, newly-built semi-detached houses with three bedrooms were selling for between £475 and £575; they are still serving that community in the south-western part of the town. Below are two small shops in Mortimer Street depicted in the 1950s. Set in houses of the 1820s they were part of a now vanished line of businesses which included a Co-op grocery store, a barber, a greengrocer, a cobbler, a clothes shop, a butcher and a post office.

IMPORTANT NOTICE

The Members of the

TROWBRIDGE, BRADFORD & MELKSHAM

BUTCHERS' ASSOCIATION

including the MULTIPLE FIRMS & CO-OPERATIVE
SOCIETIES have agreed to

CLOSE THEIR SHOPS

COMMENCING

TO-DAY, TUESDAY, FEB. 6

**as a Protest against being asked to accept
Meat which the Government has sent for
Sale to their Shops and which, in their
unanimous opinion, is Unfit for Retailing to
the Public.**

PRINTED BY B. LANSDOWN & SONS, LTD. DUKE STREET, TROWBRIDGE.

THE GOVERNMENT had taken over control of meat supplies in January 1940. A few weeks later, on Tuesday 6 February, butchers in the Trowbridge, Bradford and Melksham areas closed their shops in protest over the Government sending them meat for sale that they all felt was unfit for retail to the public. The meat in question was Uruguayan lamb, to the left of this picture of carcases in the Market House. The 200 carcases weighed only 12–15 lbs each instead of the normal 30–36 lbs and were priced 9d. (4p) a pound wholesale. The butchers said that the meat was not worth 2d. (1p) a pound and was 'not fit for dogs'. The Government had refused to release other meat unless a share of the lamb was taken but by noon on Tuesday had withdrawn the lamb which was 'not diseased but of poor quality'.

CHURCH WALK is a most interesting mixture of mainly eighteenth-century houses. The shops seen in this picture of the 1950s have changed owners and trades several times in the last 30 years.

THE WELL-STOCKED SMALL GROCERY SHOPS of the 1950s needed a bewildering variety of goods to satisfy the needs of local people. Many would deliver orders, run Christmas Clubs and even allow credit when families encountered illness and hard times.

THE 'CONIGRE STEPS' were one of the most Dickensian corners of old Trowbridge, leading down from Upper Broad Street, in front of Westcroft House, to the much lower level of Frog Lane as it turned a corner and became British Row. Who better to be photographed walking down the steps, shortly before their disappearance, than Joe Collins, bowler-hatted, double-mackintoshed, sharp-witted odd-job-man, sandwich-board-man, bicycle-cleaner, etc. – a familiar and well-loved figure in the town for over 40 years. When the steps had to go as the streets were widened and amalgamated, the town surveyor, the late Mr Geoffrey Day, preserved the old handrails, with their spiral ends, by joining them as a railing in front of the raised public seat that replaced the steps.

IT WAS THE ELDORADO 'STOP ME AND BUY ONE' TRICYCLE MAN that first introduced Trowbridge to this new way of selling ice cream, during the 1920s, but after a few years it was the name 'Walls' that appeared on the tricycles.